ZINNIE HARRIS

a new version of August Strindberg's
Miss Julie

NTS TOURING ENSEMBLE

Julie is one of the three plays in the National Theatre of Scotland's Ensemble programme for 2006. The touring company of seven actors and musicians will be performing in three productions across Scotland from late August to late October 2006.

The shows include an adaptation of a classic European play (*Julie*), a revival of a recent Scottish play (*Mancub*) and a world premiere (*Gobbo*). From Thurso in the North to Galloway in the South, the Ensemble takes residency in each community, combining performances for children, young people and adults with an ambitious workshop programme.

TOUR DATES

PLATFORM AT THE BRIDGE, EASTERHOUSE
TUE 29 AUG, 7PM
MON 4 SEP, 7PM

NORTH EDINBURGH ARTS CENTRE
FRI 8 SEP, 7.30PM

BALLACHULISH VILLAGE HALL
TUE 12 SEP, 7.30PM

MACPHAIL CENTRE, ULLAPOOL
FRI 15 SEP, 7.30PM

SABHAL MOR OSTAIG, SKYE
TUE 19 SEP, 8PM

VICTORIA HALL, CROMARTY
SAT 23 SEP, 7.30PM

THURSO HIGH SCHOOL
THU 28 SEP, 7.30PM

CRAIGMONIE CENTRE, DRUMNADROCHIT
SAT 30 SEP, 7.30PM

BETTRIDGE CENTRE, NEWTONHILL, ABERDEENSHIRE
TUE 3 OCT, 7.30PM

NEW DEER PUBLIC HALL, ABERDEENSHIRE
SAT 7 OCT, 7.30PM

TULLYNESSLE & FORBES VILLAGE HALL, NEAR ALFORD,
10 – 11 OCTOBER
WED 11 OCT, 7.30PM

THE FISHERMAN'S HALL, BUCKIE
FRI 13 OCT, 7.30PM

KIRKCOWAN VILLAGE HALL, DUMFRIES & GALLOWAY
WED 18 OCT, 7.30PM

MIDDLEBIE VILLAGE HALL, DUMFRIES & GALLOWAY
SAT 21 OCT, 7.30PM

SANQUHAR TOWN HALL, DUMFRIES & GALLOWAY
TUE 24 OCT, 7.30PM

JULIE

written by Zinnie Harris

a new version of
August Strindberg's *Miss Julie*
from a literal translation
by Hanna Slättne

CAST

John	Andy Clark
Christine	Georgina Sowerby
Julie	Samantha Young

Directed by	Zinnie Harris
Designed by	Lizzie Clachan
Lighting designed by	Kai Fischer
Music composed by	John Harris

Production Technician	Liam Boucher
Wardrobe Supervisor	Liz Boulton
Production Manager	Grahame Coyle
Workshop Director	Laura Eaurley
Assistant Stage Manager	Christine Henderson
Production Technician	Matthew Padden
Company Stage Manager	Ingrid Rochford
Deputy Stage Manager	Amy Vaughan-Spencer

Commissioned by the
National Theatre of Scotland
and first performed by the
NTS Touring Ensemble
at Platform, The Bridge,
Easterhouse, 29 August 2006

THE COMPANY

LIZZIE CLACHAN
Designer

Lizzie is a co-founder of London based Shunt. She has designed all their productions including Amato *Saltoni*, *Tropicana*, *Dance Bear Dance*, *The Tennis Show* and *The Ballad of Bobby Francois*.

Other productions include *Woman and Scarecrow* and *Ladybird* (The Royal Court), *The American Pilot* (RSC), *Bedtime Stories* and the *End of the Beginning* (The Young Vic), *Factory Girls* (The Arcola) and *Moonshed* for the Royal Exchange.

ANDY CLARK
John

Andy trained at Dundee College and RSAMD. His theatre work includes: *Roam* (NTS/ Grid Iron), *Home* (NTS), *The Devil's Larder* and *Decky Does a Bronco* (Grid Iron), *Tartuffe*, *Princess and The Goblin* (Royal Lyceum), *Baby Doll*, *A Handful of Dust*, *Cleo*, *Camping*, *Emmanuelle & Dick*, *Vernon God Little*, *The Ruffian on the Stair*, *La Musica*, *The Lady Aoi* (Citzens'), *Kidnapped* (Mull Theatre) and *Proof* (Rapture).

As a member of Dundee Rep Ensemble from 2000 to 2003 he appeared in *The Laird O'Grippy*, *The Seagull*, *Disco Pigs*, *The Winter's Tale*, *Mince*, *Pants*, *The Land O'Cakes*, *Puss in Boots*, *Caberet* and *Hansel & Gretel*.

Film and TV work includes: *Sea of Souls*, *High Times*, *Missing* and *The Da Vinci Code*.

KAI FISCHER
Lighting Designer

Kai studied Audio-Visual Media at HDM in Stuttgart. Set and lighting designs for Vanishing Point include *Lost Ones*, *Mancub*, *Glimpse*, *Blackout* and *Last Stand*. For the same company he co-directed and co-designed *Stars Beneath the Sea*, *A Brief History of Time* and *Invisible Man*. Outside Vanishing Point, Kai works as a lighting designer and recent productions include *Merlin*, *The Danny Crowe Show* (Dundee Rep), *Blood and Ice* (Royal Lyceum Edinburgh), *Switchback* (Sweetscar), *Hedda Gabler*, *Macbeth* and *A Doll's House* (Theatre Babel), *One Day All This Will Come to Nothing* (Traverse Theatre) and *Into the Dark* (Visible Fictions).

JOHN HARRIS
Composer

John's recent theatre includes: *Jerusalem* (WYP), *East Coast Chicken Supper*, *The Nest*, *Family*, *Kill the Old Torture their Young*, *Perfect Days*, *Greta*, *Knives in Hens*, *Anna Weiss*, *Sharp Shorts* (all Traverse Theatre); *Solstice*, *Midwinter* (RSC); *Il Bellissimo Silencio*, *Of Nettles and Roses*, *Stockaree* (Theatre Workshop); *Drummers* (Out of Joint). Film / TV includes: *Paternoster* (8 1/2); *The Emperor* (C4); *The Green Man of Knowledge* (S4C). John is the director of internet-based music company Seven Things and performs and writes with his multi-instrumental group SPKE.

ZINNIE HARRIS
Writer and Director

Zinnie Harris is a playwright and director. Her plays include *Solstice* and *Midwinter* (both Royal Shakespeare Company), *Nightingale and Chase* (Royal Court), *Further than the Furthest Thing* (Royal National Theatre/ Tron Theatre) winner of the Peggy Ramsay Playwriting Award and John Whiting Award, and *By Many Wounds* (Hampstead Theatre). She is currently writing for the television series *Spooks* (BBC 1/Kudos). Directing work includes *Solstice, Midwinter* (both RSC), *Gilt* (7:84), *Dealer's Choice* (Tron Theatre Company), *Master of the House* (BBC Radio Four) and *Cracked* (2001 Edinburgh Fringe First Award). She was writer in Residence at the RSC from 2000-2001.

GEORGINA SOWERBY
Christine

Georgina trained at the Drama Centre London. Theatre work includes: *The Children's Hour* (National Theatre), *Don Juan Returns From The War* (National Theatre Studio Regent's Park Open Air Theatre), *Uncle Vanya* (The Wrestling School), *Dona Rosita The Spinster* (The Almeida), *International New Writing Festival* (Royal Court), *The Cosmonauts Last Message* (The Tron), *Passing Places* (Greenwhich Theatre, Derby Playouse), *Beatrix Potter* (Unicorn Theatre), *The Sound of Silence* and *Other Rooms* (Dirty Market), *Strangers* (Oval House Theatre).

Television work includes: *Life Support* (BBC Scotland), *Poirot* (ITV), *Monarch of the Glen* (BBC) and *The Planman,* (ITV).

Georgina is co-director of Moving Arts Initiatives – creating mixed-arts events for children and Dirty Market Theatre.

AUGUST STRINDBERG

August Strindberg (1849–1912) was a Swedish dramatist, novelist, poet and essayist. His plays include *The Father* (1887), *Miss Julie* (1888), *The Stronger* (1890), *Easter* (1900), *The Dance of Death* (1900), *A Dream Play* (1902) and *The Ghost Sonata* (1907).

SAMANTHA YOUNG
Julie

Sam trained at the RSAMD. After graduating she joined Dundee Rep as part of the Graduate scheme. Plays included *Macbeth, A Lie of the Mind, The Visit* and *The Graduate*. Following this she did *A Taste of Honey* (TAG Theatre Company) and *The Crucible* (TAG / NTS). Radio credits include *Look Back In Anger, Kitty Elizabeth Must Die* and *Almost Blue* (BBC Radio 4).

[NATIONAL THEATRE OF SCOTLAND]

The National Theatre of Scotland was launched with HOME
– a theatrical event which took place in 10 locations across
Scotland, from Stornoway and Shetland to Dumfries and
Galloway, culminating with simultaneous performances on
25 February 2006. We asked ten of our leading directors to
take the word HOME as a starting point and create a piece
of theatre from it. Among the venues were shop fronts,
ferries, drill halls and tower blocks. Thousands of people
saw the work – some travelling from place to place to take
in as many events as possible. The idea was to
communicate how unique this model for a National Theatre
is and begin to show our artistic ambitions. It was about
putting directors to the fore and creating the environment
for them to take risks and to begin to push the boundaries
of our perception of theatre.

The National Theatre of Scotland has no building of its
own; there has been no great capital project involving
architects or contractors. Instead, we are creating theatre
all over Scotland, working with the existing theatres and
with the existing theatre community. We have no bricks-
and-mortar institutionalism to counter nor a safe structure
within whose walls to slowly develop. But all our money
and energy can be spent on the work on stage. Our theatre
takes place in the great buildings – the Royal Lyceum,
Edinburgh and The Citizens, Glasgow – but also in site-
specific locations, in airports, drill halls, community halls,
car parks and forests.

In our first twelve weeks of programming between
February and May 2006 we produced five major pieces of
theatre (plus our ten HOME shows), co-produced with
thirteen different companies and partners and reached out
to audiences of just over 40 000. Hundreds of people
participated in our education projects and opportunities.
This exceeded our expectations and encouraged us greatly,
In August 2006, we appeared at both the Edinburgh

International and Fringe Festivals with *Realism* and *Black Watch* respectively.

It is an interesting and often challenging task creating what will become a National Institution. As the only major publicly funded cultural institution since devolution many people have a stake in our success and we have the responsibility both to the theatre community and to the public at large to make this work. This is countered by our belief that success can only grow from encouraging artists to take risks, to surprise the audience, to be innovative and to be part of creating a forward-looking theatre not a backward-looking one. The balance is I think an interesting one which I hope creates a dynamic tension in the way we programme and develop work.

In Scotland this is particularly relevant. For better or worse, there are not hundreds of years of great weighty theatre tradition behind us which we are forced to respect. Of course there are great pieces in the canon, but there is no Shakespeare or Ibsen or Chekhov. Instead we have an extraordinary array of living playwrights including the writers working with the Ensemble – David Greig, Douglas Maxwell and Zinnie Harris.

This is a real chance to start building a new generation of theatre-goers as well as reinvigorating the existing one and to create theatre on a national and international scale that is contemporary, confident and thrilling.

I have spent many hours debating the notion of National and that responsibility. It is not nor ever should be a jingoistic, reductive stab at defining a nation's identity through theatre. It should not be an opportunity in fact to try and define anything. Instead it is the chance to throw open the doors of possibility, to encourage boldness and for audiences to benefit from where that can take us.

Vicky Featherstone
Artistic Director

*For more information about
the National Theatre of Scotland, visit*
www.nationaltheatrescotland.com
or call +44 (0) 141 221 0970

FOR THE NATIONAL THEATRE OF SCOTLAND

Scottish
Arts Council

Zinnie Harris
Julie

a new version of
Strindberg's
Miss Julie

ff

faber and faber

First published in 2006
by Faber and Faber Limited
3 Queen Square, London WC1N 3AU

Typeset by Country Setting, Kingsdown, Kent CT14 8ES
Printed in England by Bookmarque, Croydon, Surrey

A CIP record for this book
is available from the British Library

ISBN 978-0-571-23596-4
ISBN 0-571-23596-4

2 4 6 8 10 9 7 5 3 1

Characters

Julie
John
Christine

SCENE ONE

Mid-1920s. Scotland.
A kitchen.
It's late at night and hot. Sticky.
Christine is standing with a basin of water in front of her.
She takes a sponge and fills it.
She puts it to her throat and neck, cooling herself down.
She repeats, enjoying the feel of the water on her skin.
John appears at the doorway.
Christine carries on what she is doing, without turning round.

John
   Not be long now.

Christine
   You think?

John
   Aye.
      The clouds are just about ready to go. Holding on to themselves.
      There'll be thunder before the night is out.

Christine continues to wash herself.

Christine
   I'd settle for rain.

John enters the kitchen and starts to walk towards her.

Christine
   The floor is just clean.

John
   So are my feet.

He stands beside her.
He flicks her with water from the bowl. Playfully.
She thinks about it.
She flicks him back.

Christine
You've been at the dance.

John
How can you tell?

Christine
Sweat on your brow.

John
So wash it off.

She drops the sponge back in the bowl.

Christine
You do it.

John
You are bonny when you are like this.

Christine
I thought you said you weren't going.

John
I changed my mind.

Christine
Oh.

John
It's quite an event. You can hear music from halfway
across the square. It's like the circus has come to town.

Christine
It's hardly that.

John
It's a dance, Christine, that is all.

Christine

I don't know what they think they've got to dance about.

John

They are doing something to keep themselves going, that's all. Nine weeks of striking? They deserve a dance.

Christine

And when they are starving?

John

They won't starve. The boss'll cave in long before that.

Christine

Let's hope.

John

It's a new era. Solidarity, Chris, that's what these union men are saying to them. Stick together, you get what you want.

Christine

And dance while you are doing it?

John

Why not? If it helps.

Christine

Tchh.

John

I'm right behind them if you want to know.

Christine

Sure you are.

John

I was only saying just now, keep going, you'll get what you want. Hold firm.

Christine
And yet we are keeping his household going like clockwork.

John
What do you mean?

Christine
Them out there doing everything they can to put pressure on the man. Us in here, bending backwards to serve him. It's hardly –

John
It's different.

Christine
I know, I'm just saying it's –

John
We get paid more, there is no need.

Christine
Of course we do.

John
Plus we don't have a union.

Christine
Yeah.
No union.

John
And anyway, if they win we'll be the losers.

Christine shrugs.

Christine
Let's hope they win.

Beat.

Christine
Who were you with, anyway?

John
I went by myself.

Christine
Oh.

Beat.

Christine
I think it is foolish if you want to know. Really. I think they'll end up destitute and then what? He'll not give them jobs at the mill again. You know what he is like, he'll never forget, he would rather bury them all in his own graveyard before forgetting and well he might – the coffins piling up before –

John
That is how it used to be, but now – the working class, their time is coming.

Christine
We'll see.

John
We will. This mill will prove it. It will be an example.

Christine reaches for some food.

Christine
Do you want some scran or not?

John
What is it?

Christine
Bit of sausage left over from lunch.

John
Bonny.

She goes to get the food.

Christine
I'll keep the gristle on for you.

John
Any chance of a smile?

Beat.

Christine
I thought I'd have to see in the midnight sun alone.

John
I'm back the now.

Christine
So you are.

She carves the meat and puts it on a plate.

John
Julie was there.

Christine
Tell me you are joking?

John
No. She was standing at the back but when she saw me she dragged me right into the middle.

Christine
Does she know she is the boss's daughter?

John
Of course she does.

Christine
You should go back there, and bring her back. Tell her it is no place for her to be.

John
She's all right.

Christine
That crowd could turn at any second. Oh, they are dancing now but they are angry and if they can't take it out on her father –

John

No one is bothering about Julie. They are getting drunk and forgetting it all. So Julie's there dancing with her bare feet at the back, so what? She is unimportant.

Christine

She'll get a cold with no shoes on.

John

And if she does, she'll lie in bed for it just like the rest of us.

Pause.

Christine

The bread is stale, will I get another?

John

Pour me a drink with it and I'll no mind.

Christine

Beer or water?

John

Wine.

Christine

Wine?

John

There is a good burgundy just behind you.

Christine looks.

Christine

It's not ours.

John

With all this going on, you think the Lord will notice a missing bottle?

Christine

And if he does?

John

If he does, we'll say it smashed.

Christine

He'll make us pay for it.

John

So we will pay.

Christine

Or worse, the mood he is in, he –

John

It's Midsummer's Night, Chris. We work hard. Let's have a drink, eh?

Beat.

John

And in a good glass and all. Fuck it, let's have the crystal and drink to the poor buggers out there dancing their lives away. Yes?

Beat.

John

Good girl.

Christine passes him a glass.
She gets out another for herself.

John

What the hell have you done to the sausage? That never smells like sausage?

Christine

It's this that stinks. Entrails.

John

Lovely.

Christine

Don't ask.

Christine has taken the bottle of wine from the dresser.

John
   Well, open it then.

Christine opens it.

John
   When you have poured it, I'll tell you some gossip.

Christine
   What gossip?

John
   Pour it.

Christine hesitates.

John
   No gossip then.

Christine
   If he finds out –

John
   I'll say it was me, I'll blag it.

Christine
   Who is the gossip about?

John
   Couldn't possible say.

Christine pours the wine in John's glass.

John
   Julie.

Christine
   And?

John is giving nothing more.
Christine pours it into her own glass.

John
    Her young man.

Christine thinks about this. She drinks the wine.

John
    The real reason they split up.

Christine drinks again.

John
    You'll have to promise not to tell.

Christine
    Are you trying to get me drunk?

John
    Drink it.

Christine drinks again.
So does John.

John
    You won't believe it, by the way. When I tell you you'll
    only say I'm making it up.

Christine
    Is that so?

John
    You will say that I am so sordid in my mind that I had
    to go and make up stories, you'll say I had to go and
    concoct ever more fantastical tales to get your
    attention.

He looks at Christine. She looks back.

John
    All right, Chris, but you twisted my arm.
        The stable yard. Last Saturday. Miss Julie. A whip in
    her hand.
        Her fiancé down on his hands and knees.
        Both hands tied to the beam.

14

Christine chokes on the wine.

John

I told you you wouldn't believe me.

Oh come on, don't pretend you are shocked. That girl isn't the innocent that everyone thinks she is.

Should I go on or not?

Beat.

Christine

What were you doing watching?

John

I was having a smoke. I couldn't sleep so I had gone out.

I was in the wrong place at the wrong time, and what a wrong place it turned out to be.

She was flogging him, like a horse. And he was not enjoying it. This wasne about pleasure for either of them. He was begging her to stop. It was some game gone wrong I would say, some weird game if you ask me.

She had a crazed look. A line of spit on her top lip. She was not listening to his cries, not listening or not noticing, blood coming through his shirt.

It was a proper beating, Chris.

I was just about to step in, make my presence felt, when he broke the rope and tore free.

Then she looked frightened. He came over to her. Nearly knocked her sidewise. Two big blows. Sounded like he had broken her jaw.

Then he left her.

Now what the hell is all that about?

Christine

I don't know.

John

Sex? I dinne think so. Some perverted game? Nah, she was taking revenge for something. Every beating she ever got. Every time she hadn't got her way maybe. And that very evening was the one that we heard the engagement was off.

I told you you wouldn't believe it.

Christine
I don't know what to believe.

John
There is a chip in the glass, what is wrong with you tonight? Will you get me a glass that I won't cut myself on?

Christine takes the glass.
She looks at it.

Christine
Just a slight crack.

John
I'll have a new one.

Christine
And waste the wine?

John
His Lordship has plenty. I should know.

Christine drinks his wine.
John is surprised by her action. Delighted.

Christine
She is going to have to keep her head down. If His Lordship hears what she was up to, and a perfectly good young man.

John
He was a wanker.

Christine
He was fine.

John

He was hand-picked by Daddy because he would do what he was told.

Christine

Rubbish.

John

The young man's family have sway with the workers. Would have been very handy for the Lord, except Miss Julie didn't play along – or did play.

Christine

Don't laugh.

John

It's funny.

Christine

You would wipe that smile if he was here.

John

But he is not, so I can laugh.

It's an amusement to me. Julie and her dad. The strikers, the beating of a young man. A broken engagement. It's all very funny. And if the strikers get victory I'll drink with them. If they don't I'll chuck them a few coppers at Christmas. It doesn't matter. It's interesting to watch, that's all. Who knows, maybe I will ask for a pay rise next.

Christine

You would never dare.

John

I would get you to do it, then. I'd stand behind you and get you to ask. Sure there's a biting dog inside you at times.

Christine

John –

John

When you get going, when you get hot under your collar about something. Or someone.

John drinks the wine.

John

A wee tiny bit too cold. Christine, warm it if you please.

She scoffs.
But does it. She holds it to her chest, and breathes on it.

John

You will make a wonderful wife. Bit feisty maybe, but once in the sack –

Christine

You should be so lucky.

John

That is what I love about you. All spines and prickle and soft in the middle. Marry me.

Christine

God forbid.

John

Oh come off it, you love it.

Beat.

John

You are just like the wine.

He looks at the label.
He sniffs it again.

John

A wee bit too sharp but will mature nicely. Too thick for claret, but too thin for Loire. Dijon or Lausanne. There we are, we will marry in Dijon. What is that smell?

Christine
They make mustard in Dijon.

John
So you know a thing or two.

Christine
I listen.

John
Very good, even better, a wife who listens. Cooks and listens, excellent, excellent. Is something going off in here? Even entrails don't smell as bad as that?

Christine sniffs.

John
What are you up to?

Christine
I said I wouldn't say.

John
Chris?

Christine
I promised.

John
Who?

Christine
Julie.

John
Julie?

Christine
No, not really, the dog.

John
Julie's dog?

Christine
Yes.

John
She is getting you to run around after her dog now?

Christine
The dog is not well, I said I would.

John
What sort of not well?

Beat.

John
Christine. One indiscretion deserves another.

Christine
OK, but . . . the dog has been spending too much time with the gamekeeper's collie.

John
Don't they know they come from different stock?

Christine
Yeah well, spending time together wasn't all they did.

John
No . . .?

Christine
They are dogs, of course they did.
The dog was on heat, what else was the collie supposed to do?

John
Julie's dog? This is hilarious. Pups on the way?

Christine
It seems so.

John
Fantastic. First her engagement breaks down, now her dog is up the duff. Tch tch.

John laughs.

Christine
Dinne.

He laughs again.

John
And particularly with the gamekeeper's collie. It
couldn't come any better.

Christine
I know, but –

John
Tell me what are you feeding it.

Christine
Something Julie has found out about to put it all right.

John
What is she going to do, kill it?

Christine
No, just the young inside.

John
Tell me you are kidding?

Christine
What else can she do?

John
It sounds like witchcraft.

Christine
Don't say that. Don't say that word in this kitchen.
They are dogs and come from nature. Anyway, it will
all be over in a couple of hours.

John
And you will clear up the mess.

Christine
Of course I will.

Pause.

Christine
Do we have to talk about her any more? All evening
and we have only talked about her, or her dog.

John
So what shall we talk about?

Christine
I don't know.

John
Anyway I was only talking about her because –

Christine
What, Miss Julie again?

Beat.

Christine
What about a dance with me?
    If you are so desperate for a dance.
    It's midsummer as you said. It's hot. The whole mill
is dancing.

John
Sure.

Christine
Or do I need to tie you up and put a whip in my hand
for you to see me at all?

John
You never need to do that, you are grimy enough as
you are.

Christine
Oh now that is better, your attention at last.

Julie appears in the doorway. Barefoot and dishevelled. John and Christine rise respectfully.

Julie
Please don't.

They stay in their respectful positions.

Julie
Really you can both stand at ease. Carry on as if I wasn't here.

They don't move.

Julie
OK. What about the mixture, then? The dog is already in her basket.

Christine
It's ready.

John
You don't need to whisper in front of me. I'm not listening.

Julie
As if that were true.

John
Pardon me, Miss?

Julie
Nothing.

Christine shows her the poison entrail soup mixture.

Julie
Oh.

Christine
I followed the recipe.

Julie
Fine.

Christine

I'll have to open her mouth and force her. It doesn't
taste all that nice.

John

Poor mutt.

Julie

She won't know the difference.
    Once it is done, will she?

John

Of course she won't. She'll just howl and heave and
leave her babbies in a pool of blood on the floor. If you
don't mind me saying, that is, Miss.

Pause.
John smiles, all charm.

Julie

You aren't so clean yourself.

John

I wouldn't poison my own dog.

Julie

No? So what would you do?

John

I've never had a dog.

Julie

But if you did. And you found it betrayed you?

John

Betrayed?

Julie

Yes. Mixed with the lower classes. If there were lower
than you. Say it bred with a weasel or a stoat, what
then?

24

John

It's impossible.

Julie

Of course it is. A weasel or a stoat wouldn't look twice at a dog of yours, so it would be left with the rats and the vermin.

John

Have I offended you, Miss Julie?

Julie

Dance with me.

John

Again?

Julie

Why not?

John

Don't you think you have danced enough?

Julie

Surely you aren't saying you are tired of dancing.

John

No, but more than one with the same partner –

Julie

Dance is like wine, the more you drink the more you want.

John

And you have drunk too much already.

Julie

Not nearly enough.

John

Anyway, I had promised Christine.

Julie

Oh. Dance with Christine, then.

Christine
I don't mind, John.

John
But I had said.

Christine
We can postpone, can't we?
Anyway, I have to attend to the dog.

Julie
Settled.

John
Sure?

Christine
Sure.

John
Why me, Julie? Why not pick someone else this time?

Julie
You are the best dancer. It's obvious that I should dance with you, there is nothing in it.

John
But if your father were to –

Julie
Stuff my father.
He is not here, is he?
In his absence I am the Lady. You dance the best, so I will dance with you. It's just good sense, really. Who wants to stumble and fall because their partner doesn't know the steps? Not me.

Beat.

John
Who says I can dance the best?

Julie
   I don't know, it's just a rumour I heard.

They leave.
Christine watches.
She picks up the wine bottle. Rinses the glasses.
Returns the kitchen to order.
She looks at the door, the way they went.

SCENE TWO

Christine is perhaps just a little bit lonely.
She might wish she had danced after all.
She pulls a mirror out and looks at herself.
She tries putting her hair up as Miss Julie wears it.
Takes a small stub end of lipstick from her pocket and
puts it on her lips.
Miss Julie appears at the doorway.
Christine feels ridiculous. She freezes.
Julie isn't sure what to do.

Christine
   I wasn't expecting you back so soon.

Julie
   I . . .

Pause.

Julie
   I hurt my foot, that is all.

Christine
   Oh.

Julie
   Yes, there – just a small strain.
      Would you have a look at it for me?

Christine
Of course.

Julie
I tripped and fell, I don't know quite what . . .
And now my ankle.

Christine
That's a shame.

Christine has come over to her.

Christine
Which ankle?

Julie
Oh.
This one.

Christine
I thought –

Julie
No. This one.
Both really.
I was clumsy, I tripped.

Christine
I'll get something to put on it.
Something cold.

Julie
Thank you.

Pause.

Julie
I don't know what they think they are doing, having
that dance. It is still my father's mill, and he may be
away but it is blatant. They are flaunting themselves,
almost asking for the police to be called. Don't you
think?

Christine
Are you all right?

Julie
I am fine.
I am just saying, it's bad enough to refuse to work but to dance –

Christine
You have tears in your eyes.

Julie
No. It is just the pain.
My foot, I told you.

Beat.

Julie
Do you think I am foolish, Christine?

Christine
Not at all.
Why would I think that? You have hurt your foot, that is all. It can happen to anyone. I'll get you patched up and you will be as good as new.

Julie
Thank you.

Beat.
John comes in.

Julie
I'm just getting a little water. I'm thirsty.

John
Of course.
Let me get it.

Julie
Thank you, John.

He gets her a glass.

John
You look flushed.

Julie
So do you.

John
I am a little.

Julie
No wonder in that shirt.

John
That man shouldn't have said what he did.

Julie
I don't care.

John
I told him so, I went right up to him.

Julie
Change your shirt.

John
If you want I'll go back.

Julie
No. Thank you. That is the end of it.

John
He was out of order.

Julie
I don't want to hear.
Take off that shirt, John, and put on another. You will feel quite different.

John
Miss?

Julie
Take off that shirt.

John
　　What, here? In front of you.

Julie
　　Go to your room if you prefer. All I am saying is you
　　are hot, so change.
　　　　I'll close my eyes. Christine can check that I don't
　　peek.

John
　　I don't have a new one to put on.

Julie
　　But there is one of my father's right behind you.

Julie reaches for the shirt, and gives it to John.

Julie
　　If he minds, I'll say I told you to do it.
　　　　I'll say you were flushed.

John
　　It is one of his good ones.

Julie
　　So it is.

Beat.

Julie
　　What?
　　　　Dress like the Lord for the night.

John starts taking his shirt off.
Julie turns her back.
She speaks to Christine.

Julie
　　How come he doesn't mind if you see?

Christine
　　We are engaged.

Julie
    Are you?
        No one said.
        In what way are you engaged?

Christine
    The same way that you were engaged.

Julie
    I was properly engaged.

Christine
    But nothing came of it all the same.

John has finished putting the Lord's shirt on.
He turns around to Julie.

Julie
    What a transformation. You look like a real
    gentleman.

John
    Thank you.

Julie
    Until you speak.

John
    Enchanté.

Julie
    Vous parlez français?

John
    Oui – je parle français, enfin un peu.

Julie
    Un peu?

John
    Bien sûr, mais je crois que mon français est plus
    distingué que le votre.

Julie *Ah, vraiment?*

John
  Oui, mademoiselle.

Beat.

Julie
  Well, how the hell did you do that? You can't have
  been to France.

John
  How do you know?

Julie
  I thought you'd never been further than the village.

John
  I went to France and Switzerland one year.

Julie
  Don't tell me you speak Swiss too?

John
  As it happens, yes, I spent the whole summer working
  in a big hotel.

Julie
  Shame you didn't stay there.

John
  Miss Julie, are you flirting with me?

Beat.

John
  I used to watch you as a child.

Julie
  Did you really?

John
  Yes, as a matter of fact.

Julie
Please go on.

John
I couldn't possibly.

Julie
Oh, I am sure you could.

Beat.

Julie
Should I twist your arm?

John looks at Christine, who is falling asleep in a chair.

John
Well, look at her. Completely done in.

Julie
Congratulations, by the way, you didn't tell me you
were engaged.
I am sure she will make you a pleasant wife.
A pleasant snoring wife.

John
She isn't snoring.

Julie
Oh, it sounds like snoring.

John
It may sound that way, but it isn't.

Julie
So what is it, then?

They listen to her.

John
It's talking.

Julie
Is it really.

John
Yes it is.

Julie
I've never heard it called that before.

John
There are words in there, if you listen.

Julie
So what is she saying, then?

John
'Careful, John. Careful. Careful.'

Pause, during which they study each other.

Julie
Why don't you sit down?

John
Because it wouldn't be right to sit down with you.

Julie
But if I tell you too?

John
Then of course I will sit.

Julie
All right, sit.
    And get me something to drink.

John
There is only beer down here.

Julie
Beer is fine. I prefer it actually.

*John takes a bottle of beer from the ice box and opens it.
He get a glass from the cupboard and serves her.*

John
Allow me.

Julie
OK.
What about you?

John
I don't prefer beer.
Unless you are telling me to prefer it.

Julie
Bloody well sit down and drink it with me, you sod.
We haven't spoken for ages.

John
We speak all the time.

He gets out another beer and takes out a glass.

Julie
Your health.

John
Thank you.

He drinks.

Julie
And mine?

John
Sorry.

He gets down and kneels with mock solemnity and raises his glass.

John
Your very good health, and all that may sail in you.

Beat.

John
What? That is what they say.

Julie
Kiss my shoe, then. Make the moment perfect.

John hesitates a moment, then he takes hold of her foot and touches it lightly with his lips.

Julie
You should have been on the stage.

John
That is enough.

Julie
What?

John
I shouldn't have done that. I am sorry.

Julie
Don't be crazy. I liked it.

John
You know what is going on here as well as I do.

Beat.

Julie
But we aren't alone. Christine is with us.
If you are uncomfortable being alone with me, I'll wake her.

John
No.

Julie
Christine, wake up.

John
Don't.

Julie
Christine.

John
I said stop it.

He comes over and stops her.

John
She works hard, she deserves her sleep.

Pause.
Christine has in fact woken up.
She opens her eyes, she looks at them both.

John
Shush. It is nothing.

Christine
What about the bell?

John
You are dreaming.

Christine
His Lordship is ringing the bell . . .

John
Fantasy.

Christine
It rings and rings all day and never stops.

John
No bell.

Christine looks from him to Miss Julie.

Christine
No bell?

She stands up.

John
Sleep, sweetheart. Go to bed and sleep.

Christine scratches her head.
She walks out.

Julie
So long, Christine.

John
You should go to bed too.

Julie
Maybe I should.

Beat.

Julie
What? You can't possibly think that I am fond of my father's attendant. Not even you.

John
It isn't what I think that matters. It is what your father would think.

Julie
It happens all over the land.

John
It doesn't happen here.
Or when it does it is the talk of the village.

Julie
Not at the moment, no one is talking about anything but the strike.

John
Take my advice, Miss Julie, don't even think about it – even if it is only thought, it will take you more than that to get your reputation back.

Julie
You don't think much of them, these talkers.

John
I didn't say that.

Julie
You look down on them.

John
Maybe I do.

Julie
And me, you look down on me.

John
How can I do that?

Beat.

Julie
You remind me of a dream. If you must know.

John
Oh.

Julie
It's a recurring nightmare actually.

I am standing on top of a building. The church in fact. I'm really high, looking over the village, on top of the spire, and I can see everyone and everything but they can't see me. I am invisible almost. Then I realise I don't know the way down. I don't even know how I got up or what I am doing up there. I turn around to see whether there was a ladder or a rope bridge or even an open window that I climbed out of, but there isn't. I am stuck basically, up there miles away from the ground. Everyone is going about their day-to-day but I can't even attract their attention. I try to scream but they don't hear. I am going to either have to stay up there for ever and rot, or I am going to have to jump.

John
How awful.

Julie
Only say it like that if you mean it.

John
I do mean it.

Julie
It's a long way down.

John
So what do you do?

Julie
I do jump, actually. In the end.

John
You do?

Julie
Yes. After a bit more screaming and still no one hearing, yes, I tuck my dress into my knickers and jump.

John
All the way?

Julie
All the way.

John
And what happens as you get to the bottom?

Julie shrugs.

Julie
I'm awake by then.

John
Funny, my dreams are the opposite.

Julie
Oh?

John
Exactly the opposite. I am climbing. Isn't that interesting?

Julie
Very.

John
I am standing looking up at a tall tree in the wood, the little bit of woodland on the far side of the road. I see

that there is a bird's nest at the top of the tree, just a bit out of reach behind the branches. And so I start to climb, and I climb and climb, every branch I tread onto, the nest is still just a little out of reach, but it is getting closer. And closer. And then I am almost upon it and I can see the little eggs sitting so vulnerable in the nest.

Julie
Then what happens?

John
I wake up. Just like you.

Julie
Oh.

John
I suppose it is like the landing in yours, it doesn't quite happen.
Or it hasn't happened yet.
The brain stops it before the final beat.

Julie
You wake up with a start?

John
I wake up covered in sweat.

Julie
I am surprised, I would have expected you to have grabbed the little eggs and eaten them whole, crunched and chewed and spat out the gristle.

John
I'll try that, next time I am asleep.
Do you hate me?

Julie
Not at all.

Beat.

John
They say that if you wash your face with the dew on
Midsummer's Night your dreams will come true.

Beat.

Julie
You've got something in your eye.

John
No I haven't.

Julie
A black streak.
A sort of blob.

John
Where?

Julie
Just in the corner.

John
Rubbish.

Julie
I'll get it out for you.

John
I'm fine.

Julie
It must have been my sleeve a moment ago.

John
Get off.
There is nothing there – ow!

Julie
I told you.

John
Well, it wasn't there a second – ouch!

Julie
Let me look.

John
I don't know what it is.

Julie
Come here.

Julie takes him by the arm and makes him sit down; takes hold of his head and bends it backwards; tries to get the dirt with a corner of her handkerchief.

Julie
Well, you have to stay still.

Julie slaps him on the hand.

Julie
Still. What is wrong with you, you are shaking.

John
Miss Julie.

Julie
Yes, Monsieur John.

Beat.

Julie
Sit still, I said, do you want to be blinded by this thing?
There, got it. A black blob, I told you.

John
Thank you.

Julie
Is that all?

John
Listen to me, Christine has gone to bed.

Julie
Kiss my hand.

John

What are you doing?

Julie

Nothing.

John

Don't pretend you're naive.

Julie

I don't know what you are talking about.

John

You are playing with fire.

Julie

I wish I was.

It seems more like I am playing with a bucket of cold water.

John kisses her on the lips.

Julie

How dare you? I said my hand.

John

What is it now, more play?

Julie

That wasn't play.

John

Then neither is this.

He kisses her again.

John

And now I am tired of playing. I have to get up early unlike some. Your father is back tomorrow and he will want everything in order and I need to be up before the house is awake and it is nearly midnight.

Julie

Don't go.

She pulls him to her and kisses him.

John
> I don't want to play any more.
>> I am not going to amuse you any more.
>> You are teasing me, and I don't like it.

Julie
> Have you ever loved?

John
> No.

Julie
> Oh.

John
> Why would I waste my time with all that shit?

Beat.

John
> OK, not love, I wouldn't call it that. But I have made myself sick with longing.

Julie
> How sick?

John
> Couldn't eat, couldn't drink.

Julie
> That is it.
>> So you do know love.

John
> No.

Julie
> Of course that's love, how else does it manifest itself?

John
> All right, that might be what the posh call it.
>> I call it an illness. A virus.

Julie
Who was it?

Pause.

Julie
Who was it, that you loved?

John
Just some lass.

Julie
A girl from the village?

John
In a way.

Julie
Did she know?

John
Never.

Julie
Was she married?

John
She was engaged, then broke it off.

Julie
Then you should tell her.

Beat.

John
Maybe.

Julie
Tell me about how sick you felt.
Don't spare the details, I don't mind.

John
Why should I?

47

Julie
Because I am interested.
Because we are friends.

John
Rotten to the core.
If you want to know.
All I could think about was her.
Her body, how she moved.
Catching glimpses of her flesh beneath her clothes.
I wanted to spy on her all day. I closed my eyes and imagined I was kissing her, wherever I went I saw her body in front of me, and found myself writhing with her in my sleep and waking up and saying her name over and over.

Julie
Which name?

John
Yours.

Julie
Stop it, you are mocking me.

John
No.

Beat.

John
Julie Julie and again Julie Julie.

Beat.

Julie
How weird.

John
Ludicrous even.
Julie Julie.
I imagined I had tens of thousands of Julies all

48

around me, every way I turned, her face, her shoulders, her arms, her breasts, her thighs.

Julie

Stop it.

John

Anyway, I beat myself out of it.
It was ridiculous. I soon realised.

Julie

So you loved me?

John

It was awful, I wanted to die.
First I ran to the station and spent the night sitting on the tracks, then when the train didn't come I got myself wet through and drank myself stupid. I was sure I was going to be dead by the morning.

Julie

You wanted to be dead?

John

Of course I did.

Julie

And all for me?

John

No. For despair of being me. It was a virus, I told you.

Julie

You tell such a good tale. You should be an entertainer. A showman.

John laughs.

John

Maybe.

Julie

Kiss me again.

John
  And ignite all that again. I would rather die.

John nearly does, then thinks about it.

John
  I got over you, Julie.

Julie
  I am lonely.

John
  I know you are.

Julie
  I have had a fucking awful week.

Beat.

Julie
  Let's climb to the top of the mill and watch the sunrise.

John
  Julie, you have to stop this.

Julie
  I've got a key.

John
  I can't.

Julie
  It sounds like you are more worried about your
  reputation, your job. What my father would think of
  you.

John
  Aye, maybe, I don't want to be made to look
  ridiculous.
    Poor sad John thought he could love the Lord's
  daughter, in fact was sacked without so much as a
  reference.

Julie

I'll give you a reference.

John

After your father has made sure I will never work again.

And then there is Christine.

Julie

So it is Christine now.

John

Yes, Christine, me, you, all of us. None of us will end up the better for this. I am protecting myself.

He kisses her again.

John

Go to bed, Julie.

Julie

Is that an order?

John

Yes.

Plus that sounded like someone outside. It could be Clara or one of the washgirls coming back from the dance.

Don't let them find you here.

Julie

Me, or you?

John

You.

Julie

Why not? They always say they love me. Most of them have known me since I was born.

John

Yes, they say it, of course they do, but they don't mean it. They have to say that because your father pays them. They hate you, if you want to know, behind your back they scorn. They laughed and laughed when they heard your engagement was off. The gardener sat here and opened a bottle of beer to celebrate your misfortune.

Julie
I don't believe it.

John
Seeing you and me together would keep them going for weeks.
And don't think they would keep it to themselves, your father would hear for sure.

Julie
He wouldn't believe it.

John
Maybe, maybe not.

Beat.

John
But what if it's not Clara? What if it is one of the mill workers? They don't love, and right now they aren't even getting paid. You heard what they were chanting at you at the dance, you saw the hatred in their faces –

Julie
I said I didn't want to hear about that again tonight.

Julie hears something outside.

Julie
Someone is in the garden. They are through the gate.

John
Keep away from the window.

Julie
Can you see their face?

John

No, but stand back, don't let them see yours.

Julie

I'll have to get back upstairs.

John

Go through my room.

Julie

Yours?

John

It leads straight to the stair.

Julie

The very place you didn't want me to go.

John

You can hide in there until they are on their way, that is all I am saying.

Julie

Then I will go straight back up the stair.

John

Of course you will.

Julie

Do you promise?

There is a crash outside.

John

We need to get you out of here.

Julie

You didn't answer me.

John

I can't, can I? We go into my room, and what? We don't touch? I can't promise –

Julie
But I can. We don't touch.

Beat.

John
Very well.
We don't touch.

Julie goes out towards John's room.
John follows.

SCENE THREE

A little time later.
It's now almost dawn.
Julie comes back in. She sits down on a chair.
She plays with the water.
She is half-dressed.
John comes in.
John
OK?

Julie
Yes.

He smiles.

John
I thought you were sleeping.

Julie
I was. No, I wasn't. I tried, I . . .
You were sleeping.

He brushes her hand.

John
Sorry.

Julie
No need.

John
Sure you're . . .

Julie
Fine.

They kiss.

John
I didn't know you were so . . .

Beat.

John
Different. You are different. Beautiful different.
Wonderful different.

Julie
I didn't know you were . . .

John
Come on, that was your first time.

Julie
Maybe.

John
Nothing to be ashamed of.

Julie
How do you know?

John
I know. I mean, I'm not saying you didn't get into your
stride but . . .

He comes over to her.

John
Let me dress you.

Julie

You don't need to.

John

I want to. I want to keep touching you. I don't want to wake up and have the spell broken.

He puts one of her stockings on her leg.

John

Beautiful gorgeous legs. I could kiss them all day.

He starts putting on the other stocking.

Julie

Stop.

John

Don't say that.

Julie

Someone has broken in. My things, someone has moved them. Your glass. The plate. The table. Whoever it was, did come in.

John looks around.

John

The window blew open, that's all.

Julie

Someone has been here.

John

It will have been Clara or Jacob.

Julie

I don't care who it was, don't you see – they probably –

John

What?

Julie

Heard.

Beat.

Julie
How thick is the wall between your room and here?

John
Thin.

Julie
So if someone were to stand where I am standing –

John
They'd hear everything.

Julie
Shit.

John
Don't worry about it.

Julie
Don't worry about it?

John
We'll think of something.
We knew we were taking a risk. So we were a little noisy.
What did we expect?

Julie looks around.

John
I'll find out who it was, slip them a pound or two.

Julie
It will be right round the village.

Pause.

John
OK. I have a friend in London. He works on the ferries. He can get us a pass. That is what we will do. We'll go to Belgium, France, Austria or somewhere.

Go abroad for a little while. A couple of weeks, let the scandal run its course.

Julie
Don't you read the newspapers? The ferries are striking as well.

John
All right, so not a ferry.

Julie
Everyone is striking.

John
I'll drive us if I have to. So there is a strike everywhere. That's good. Everyone will be preoccupied. We'll start a hotel. Everyone else is striking, so we'll work. We'll make a fortune.

Julie
This is madness.

John
Why?
    A hotel for posh bods, like you. You'll be the poshest thing in it.

Julie
What do you mean, we will work?

John
I'll work. You will be just for show. You will be the measure of class, letting people in and out the door. Hotels are where it is at. The money that passes through the door in places like that.

Julie
We won't get far, it's ridiculous.

John
We'll get as far as Glasgow, just away from here is all we need. Ireland – how about Ireland?

Julie

You are crazy.

Beat.

John

Listen, I love you. It will be OK.

Maybe not Ireland and maybe not a hotel, but it will be OK.

Julie

Say it again.

John

Which bit?

Julie

The first bit.

John

The bit about maybe not Ireland?

Julie

No, the bit before that.

John

You come with me and I will say it every night and every morning.

Julie

Say it now.

John

I love you.

Julie

And again?

John

We need to think about how we can get out of here. What time the coach leaves for London.

Julie

The coach?

John

If you are serious we will have to get going.

Julie

Are you serious?

John

Of course I am.

Julie

Take me in your arms then.

John

There is time enough for that.

Julie

Show me.

John

We need to get dressed. Julie, put your clothes on.

Julie

YOU PUT THEM ON.

Beat.

John

I want to, of course I do. You can't doubt that, but we need to get moving, Miss Julie, while we are in this house.

Julie

Miss?

John

A habit. Julie.

No, I can't do it. That is why we need to get away. As long as we are in this house you are Miss Julie and I am the staff. Your father's attendant. Nothing much. In Ireland you'll see another man in me, but here – we need to get away. Just standing in this kitchen and I feel my resolve going. Step outside with me, I'll show you who I am. On that ferry, or that hotel . . . You can buy a title in Ireland, by the way. So they say. When we have made a little of ourselves, we will become lords. How would you like that? A lady?

Julie
I am a lady.

John
A countess then. My countess.

Julie
Yours?

John
Of course mine. You wouldn't be your father's any longer.

Julie
Call me Julie like you did before.

John
Julie.

Julie
Put your arms around me. Please.

Beat.
He does.
But it is quick. Too quick.
He sees her disappointment.

John
We need to be level-headed, keep moving forward.

Julie
Level-headed?

John
Yes, we need to think through this situation, our escape, we need to plan the operation.

Julie
This isn't an operation.

John

Listen, there is nothing I would like more, but . . .

Julie

But what?

John

We have made one mistake. Let's not make another.

Julie

Am I a mistake to you?

John

No, the time with you was –

Yes, all right, it was a mistake. To do it here, with your father about to come home any moment. What do you want me to do, make love to you again on this floor?

Julie

If you wanted.

John

We don't have any time, Julie.

Julie

Where are you getting the money? Two coach tickets to the west coast. The passages across to Ireland, let alone the capital to buy the hotel.

John

I am not a scrounger, if that is what you are implying. I have means.

Julie

And what are they?

John

My wits.

My expertise.

My ideas.

Julie
It won't even buy you the coach fare.

John
So I will need someone to come in with me.

Julie
And who would that be?

Beat.

John
Forget it.

Julie
I didn't say that.

Beat.

Julie
You know if I had it –

John
You don't have it?

Julie
I have an allowance.

John
And how far would that get us?

Julie
To the end of the drive.

Beat.

Julie
Sorry, but if I had known you were counting on it –

John
It's off then.

Julie
What?
That is it?

John
    Pretty much.

Julie
    So we stay here and let them point the finger at us?

John
    I wouldn't worry about it.
        We had a screw. It happens.

Beat.

Julie
    Is that all it was?

John shrugs.

John
    Have a glass of wine with me.

Julie
    Stolen wine.

John
    Don't, then. Suit yourself. I'll drink it. You can pour.

Julie
    Me serve you?

John
    It is hard to see you as the same lady – yes, to me, now
    you aren't who you were yesterday.

Julie
    What do you mean by that?

John
    The things you did.

Julie
    You didn't mind.

John
    Of course I didn't, who would, but they change things.

Julie

Shut up. Don't you ever say that again, if you had any idea how much I regret –

John

Regret? You wanted to go round again. A moment ago you were begging for more.

Julie

You are just a servant.

John

And you are just a screw.

Beat.

John

All right, that was too harsh.

Julie

You said you loved me.

John

I do, in my way. Listen I would have said anything to get into your knickers, you have to understand that.

Julie

Afterwards. You said it afterwards.

John

I wanted your money then. You know what kind of an animal a woman is. I had to give you something.

Julie

Charlatan.

John

And in English?

Julie

Scoundrel.
    Thief, liar.

John
Get it all out.

Julie
Was there any of what you said to me that I can trust?

John
Not much.

Julie
You are filthy.

John
Not as filthy as you.

Julie
I feel contaminated. Every part of me that has been touched.

John
So wash.

He chucks a sponge at her.

Julie
You wash.

Julie chucks it back at him.

John
No, you wash first.

He hurls it with real violence. Water is all over the floor.

Julie
You will not get away with this. I am the mistress of the house. Will you look at me when I am talking to you?

John looks at her.

Julie
You are a servant.

John

And you are a servant's fuck. Now which is worse?
You tell me I am filthy, what about you? Wasn't it you
that was begging to get into my bed, and that is not all
that you begged for. You think that women of my class
act the way you did? Oh, I am not saying I didn't
enjoy it – but don't you have the nerve to tell me that
I am vulgar. You offered the dish, I took it.

Julie

Oh God.

John

To be honest, it was too easily offered to be all that
tasty. I prefer women who hold a little back in reserve.

Julie

Why don't you hit me in the face and be done with it?

Beat.

John

You disappoint me, that's all.

Julie

You talk as if you are already above me. What, am I
dancing to your tune now?

John

I could have made a countess of you, but you could
never have made me a count.

Julie

No, but I have no need of a title, unlike you.

John

We all need titles.

Julie

Let thief be yours, then. Thief and liar.

John

There are worse things.

Julie
Not to my mind.

Beat.

John
We made a mistake. Can't we leave it at that?

Julie
That word again.

John
OK, at the time not a mistake, but Julie –

Julie
So it is Julie now?

John
Look at us. You. Me. It wouldn't work. In another universe maybe.

Julie
Don't be nice to me now.

John
You are beautiful, smart – of course in another lifetime –

Julie
Don't talk like that, you won't win me round.

John
I don't know how to talk to you. You don't want the harsh truth, you don't want the sweet lies – what do you want?

Julie
Talk to me as you would to Christine.

John
It's different with Christine.

Julie
How is it different?

Beat.

Julie
Don't tell me, she is a real lady?

John
No.

Julie
She keeps herself in reserve?

John
No. You are nothing like her.

Julie
You treat her like an equal. You don't give her bullshit.
I've heard you. You are completely yourself.

John
I don't know you like I know her.

Julie
So get to know me.

John
Don't do that, don't suck me back in.

Julie
We are talking frankly now, aren't we? We are in this
together. Whether we are running away or staying to
face the music, it's happened. That won't change.

John
I didn't steal your father's wine. It was a corked bottle.
I opened it.

Julie
Whatever. It is vulgar to drink anyway. Apparently.

Julie holds our her glass.

Julie
Are we friends or not?

John
  I don't know.

Julie
  Oh for God's sake.

John
  OK, friends like those of childhood. Not to be relied
  on.

Julie
  Fine, childhood chums.

She drinks back her glass.

Julie
  Have you fucked Christine?

John
  It's none of your business.

Julie
  She looks like a horse.

John
  Charming.

Julie
  I don't see how you could have fucked her.

John
  Julie?

Julie
  What?
  We have no secrets. We are childhood friends.
  Playmates. Full of childish things and giggling together
  in corners. You know what I think? She doesn't let you
  fuck her. Not until you are wed. Oh she lets you look
  and that might be enough to drive you crazy, but try to
  touch and you get your fingers cut off with that
  carving knife of hers.

John
Think what you like.

Julie
Either that or you don't want to. You get halfway but the stench of that day's cooking turns your stomach and you have to jump off.

John
Now I feel like striking you.

Julie
Go ahead.

Pause.

Julie
I should have been a man. By the way. I wish I was sometimes. If I was a man I would take a gun and put it to your head. Oh, I wouldn't shoot, I would just hold it there for one, two, three seconds. Enough to see you shake.

'HAVE YOU FUCKED CHRISTINE?' I would say. And you would answer . . . ?

Beat.

John
No.

Julie
Oh.

Beat.

Julie
So she drives you crazy, then.

John
She keeps her virtue.

Julie
She is a tease.

John

You have lost your gun.

Julie

Don't think I wouldn't know how to use it. Don't think I wouldn't have pre-loaded it and cleaned out the barrel. I would sneak in, late at night, behind your back while you were polishing boots or scraping some crap.

John

I don't scrape crap.

Julie

I am holding the gun, you scrape crap. I have killed, by the way. The first time when I was only six. My mother put the gun into my hand and sent me out on a shoot. 'Julie – off you go, come back with blood on your trousers and be the boy I want you to be.'

'Yes, Mama.'

And so after the rabbit, shot at blank range, came the pig and then the horse with the broken leg. All the time my father away and not knowing how his little girl was being groomed into an heir.

'A woman is every bit as good as a man. In fact better,' she would say to me. 'And you will be the best of all. Julie, you are the best of all.' What?

John

Nothing.

Julie

You scorn.

John

She was a little unusual, your mum.

Julie

She saved this family.

John

Of course she did.

Julie

The insurance money? Where would we be without her.

John

What insurance?

Julie

After the fire, we would have lost the mill if it hadn't have been for her.

John

Your father had money.

Julie

Not much, and he hadn't paid his premiums – he would have lost it all. But my mother, with her practical quick wit, arranged it.

John

She slept with the builder.

Julie

She was resourceful. She had a lover, who she now used.

John

That is one way of putting it.

Julie

What was she supposed to do, see the whole estate sold off? My father lose everything?

John

She might as well have, he didn't thank her for it.

Julie

He did in his way.

John
Oh come on, he paid her out for it.

Julie
He found it difficult to be in her debt.

John
More than difficult. We all heard the beatings.

Julie
He can be a monster when he wants to be, we all know that.

John
I thought you took his side anyway, always running along behind him like a little lap dog.

Julie
She was dead by then.

John
So he beat you too.

Julie
I look too like her, that is what he said. I carry her spirit, and lucky I do because I won't let what happened to her, happen to me.

John
And what is that?

Julie
Become a slave to a man.
    Get married only to have your wings clipped.

John
So that is why you got engaged.

Julie
That is why I broke it off.

John
He broke it off.

Julie
When he knew I wasn't that sort of a woman.

John
When he knew what sort of woman you were.

Julie
Anyway, how did you know he broke it off?

John
I saw it.

Julie
You spied on me?

John
You could call it that.
I saw the whole spectacle.

Julie
It wasn't a spectacle. He was a scoundrel, I saw him off.

John
So you did.

Beat.

Julie
I did.

John
I'm sure you did.

Beat.

Julie
To think I liked you. Now I despise you . . .

John
I think I'll live.

Julie
I'd put you out in the street like rubbish.
I'd drown you in a bucket like a rat.

John

    I preferred the first one.

Julie

    I'd put my bare hands around you and strangle you like a kitten.

John

    But I am not a kitten, a rat or a bag of rubbish. So what shall we do?

Julie

    Go abroad.

John

    And strangle each other there?

Julie

    Screw ourselves senseless first.

John

    It's an idea.

Julie

    Then scratch each other's eyes out.

John

    Perfect.
        But right now, I'm tired.
        You won't mind if I go to bed?

Julie

    And that is it?

John

    What more do you want?
        We have stayed up half the night together.
        We have told each other that we love each other, and that we hate each other. We have done what takes many couples thirty years to achieve. I am going to bed.

Julie
Let's see in the dawn.

John
I'm really sleepy.

Julie
So – what? Just a yawn and that is it, you are off?

John
Pretty much.

Julie
You owe me more than that.

John
Oh, it is money you want. Help yourself.

He throws her a coin.

Julie
You sod.
   I can't believe what I have done. I can't imagine what came over me.

John
I don't know what you want. Julie? What is this? Me to weep like you? Jump over your whip? Lure you away with false promises? I can't. I don't feel the way you do. You want the truth, Julie, I don't feel much at all. I don't exactly hate you, but I am a long way off anything you call affection. Mild affection maybe, like for a dog that has a poor leg.

Julie
And that is it?

John
I am afraid it is.
   I didn't pretend anything else. I told you I was over you. Every move that was made here tonight you made first.

Julie

You said you loved me.

John

Did I? I don't remember. Was I inside you when I said it?

Julie

You won't survive here. You disgrace me. I'll disgrace you. I'll say it was all your doing, I'll crawl up on Daddy's knee and tell him what his evil favourite servant did.

John

He won't believe it.

Julie

I'll tell him I screamed out but you didn't stop.

John

I'll tell him I screamed out but you didn't stop.

Julie

He'll break your back.

John

He'd have to catch me first.

Julie

He'll use his contacts. He'd hound you. I'll stitch you up. Last week thirty pounds went from the office drawer. I'll say it was you. He'll make sure you hang for theft. My father turns against you, and you don't stand a chance.

John

And what about you? He turns against you –

Julie

He will never turn against me.

John

I'll find Clara, or the gardener or whoever it was who came in the kitchen door and, who knows, maybe they even opened the door to my room, so intrigued by the noise, and there they saw you with your dress around your ankles and your tits out. A full description from the crowd should be the end of it. You won't be Daddy's princess any more.

Alternatively.

Neither of us say anything. I pay a few of the staff off to keep silent. And we go on as if nothing happened.

Julie

And if it happens again?

John

It won't.

Julie

Impossible.

Beat.

John

OK.

It's three hours until the coach goes. I'll give you a lift.

You have friends in Glasgow, don't you?

Julie

Why must I go? This is my home.

John

Because he is your father. If I were to go, he would guess why, then we would both be sunk. He is in no mood for disobedience and scandal. I'll deny all, there are ten men on this estate and it could be any of us.

Julie

And the witness?

John

The witness won't breathe a word against me. We stick together, us menials.

Julie

Come with me.

John

It wouldn't work.

Can you imagine the scene? Your father arrives back, you and me are missing. He would tear up the country trying to find us.

Julie

I am too tired.

John

That is why I'm going to drive you to the coach. Go up and dress. Get a bag together, come back down.

Julie

Come up with me?

John

To your room? Don't be absurd. You are speaking shamefully now.

Julie

And you are ordering me about.

John

Yes, call it a novelty.

Go.

Julie goes out.
John is alone for a second.
He takes the cloth and mops up the spilt water from the floor.
Christine enters, dressed for church.
She sees John on his hands and knees with the cloth.
She comes over and takes the cloth out of his hands.
She mops the water.
They don't speak for a few seconds.

Christine

What has happened here?

John
Oh, a bit of a party.

Christine
What sort of a party?

John
Julie brought all of the staff in here. You must have slept through it all.

Christine
I suppose I must.
Are you ready?

John
What for?

Christine
It's Sunday.

John
Already?

Christine
It normally follows Saturday, John.

John
I meant it is the morning so soon.

Christine
It is already half-nine.
Have you been to bed at all?

John
Yes, I've been to bed.

Christine
Then you are refreshed. Off we go.

John
I am not ready.

Christine
I can see that.
Don't treat me as an idiot, John.

Beat.

John
What do you want me to say?

Christine
That it is as you told me, the staff came in for a drink.

Beat.

Christine
Oh God.
I hope you know what you are doing?

John
Is that it, no cry of jealousy, no attempt to scratch my eyes out?

Christine
It is her that I feel sorry for.

John
Is that all?

Christine
You are disgusting.

John
That's a start.

Christine
You are a disgusting swine. You know she is not herself, one only needed to look at her yesterday to see she was on some kind of self-destruct mission. But you couldne leave it, could you? You had to go in there for the kill.

John
She said she enjoyed it.

Christine

Please spare me the details.

John

It may surprise you, but she enjoyed it quite a lot.

Christine

JOHN!

Beat.

Christine

I'll go to church alone. And when I get back I will
pack up my stuff. I can't stay here now.

John

It was just a fuck.

Christine

Don't say that.
  You shouldn't have done it.

John

What about her?

Christine

It isn't about her. You, you were the one that should
have known better. It isn't right, John, they are our
employers, you don't just go.

John

You hate them as much as I do.

Christine

But that doesn't mean I want to bring the whole thing
down. Yes, I hate the fetching and the carrying and the
answering the blessed bell, but it doesn't mean I would
have it any other way. We are better with the devil we
know.

John

So you will stay as the underdog.

Christine

I am the underdog. I was born it, and will always be –

John

That's crap. There is no such thing as what you are born. What, the make-up of your blood is different? The sinews in your veins? Theirs say 'servant' and hers say 'lady'?

Christine

I don't know about biology.

John

Then learn. We are all born the same. It's luck where you end up. Julie and I were born in the same hospital in the same week. She was taken home in a Silver Cross pram and I was carried in a beige blanket. That is all there is.

Christine

All I know is that this is the system we have got. We may not like it, but that is all we have. We eat, don't we? We don't starve. We have a roof over our heads. That is enough for me. You pull all this down, and what are we left with?

John

Something better.

Christine

No. A new version of exactly the same.
There will always be the underdog, John.

John

But it won't include me.

Christine

Fine, off you go. Bugger off and make your fortune. See how far you get.

John

I will walk you to church.

Christine

I can go alone.

Beat.

Christine

By the way, when I was dressing a call came. The Lord
is on his way home already.

John

What?

Christine

He is about an hour away.

John

You didn't tell me.

Christine

There were other things on my mind.

John

He is supposed not to be back until this afternoon.

Christine

The talks must have either ended or broken down.
An hour or so, John, two at most.
You know you look almost frightened.
Who has been caught with their hand in the pantry?
Where have all your thoughts of revolution gone now?

John

Shut up.

Christine

I just hope you know what you are doing.

Christine exits.
John is still wearing the Lord's shirt from the night
before. He takes it off hurriedly.
He folds it and hangs it up.
He tries to smooth the creases.

Julie enters in a travelling dress and carrying a small birdcage covered with a sheet.
John indicates that someone else is in earshot.

John
Shush.

Julie
Who?

John
Christine.

Julie
Virgin Mary herself.

John
Enough.

Julie
How do I look?

John
Terrible.

Julie
Thanks.

John
Your mascara has run.

Julie
It's OK.
I'll do it.
I got some money, by the way.

John
Where from?

Julie
Daddy's drawer.

John
There isn't much there.

Julie

So you've seen it?

John

I may have peeked in, in passing.

Julie

Then you'll know there is a key.
> And the key opens a side panel at the back.
> And in there . . .

She shows him some money.

Julie

. . . is more than you can imagine.

John

Bloody hell.

Julie

Enough?

John

Enough, I should say.

Julie

Come with me. A woman travelling alone with this much money? It won't do.

John buttons up his shirt.
He looks at the money.

John

We would have to go straight away.
> No hesitation, nothing.

Julie

OK.

John

Your father is on his way home.

Julie

Fine. How long have we got?

John

Moments only, an hour at most.

We can't take any luggage. Just what we are dressed in.

Julie

I understand.

Beat.

John

What the hell is that?

Julie

The only thing I need.

John

You'll have me.

Julie

I can't leave it behind.

John

You are running away with your lover, but taking your pet bird?

Julie

It's a finch.

John

It's a bird.

And it will squawk.

Julie

It never squawks.

John

Julie? Are you mad?

Julie

Quite insane.

Beat.

Julie
First squawk, and it's on its way out.

John
No.
It's him or me.

Julie
What? It's the only memento of my home.

John
Too bad.

Julie
Kill it then. I'd rather you killed it than we left it here.

John
Sure, I'll wring its neck.

Julie
Are you joking?

John
Are you?

Beat.
Julie takes the bird out.

Julie
Never more serious.

She gives him the bird.
He breaks its neck.

John
Oh, come on. What happened to the girl who killed a dog, aged six?

Julie
Kill me too.
You seem to have such ease.
What is the value of one life over another?
Pulp my brains like you did his.

John

You'd take longer.

Plus you'd scream.

Julie

Cold-blooded monster.

John

You told me to do it.

Julie

I didn't think you would.

She holds the dead bird.

Julie

Don't think because I flinched that I am weak. Don't think that if I was so commanded I wouldn't take an axe and do for you like you did for him. Three blows should do it, one across the back of the neck, then the torso, last of all the head. Then as you fell on the floor I would take my shoes off and bathe my feet in your warm blood, reach down, take your still beating heart out and hold it as it died.

Just because I wanted you doesn't mean anything. Just because I gave in to lust doesn't mean I want to have any more to do with you – and running away doesn't mean I am a coward either by the way. In fact, what if I don't run away? What if I stay? Stay here while my father arrives home and finds the money gone?

Stand by as he rings the bell for his favourite butler? Then the police.

And then I shall tell him how I was commanded to do it. He will find it hard to hear but will listen like a good man, then will fall down dead from the weight of a broken heart. And that will be the end of it.

You to the gallows.

My father to the grave.

And your evil progeny, already fostering itself in my womb.

John
Very good.
He'll grow up to write his memoirs and win an award.

Julie
Shut up.

Christine comes in, still dressed for church and with her prayer book.

Julie
Thank God.
Christine, you have to help me.

Christine makes no attempt to help her.
She sees the dead bird.

Christine
What the hell is this?
And on a Sunday.

Julie
He is a dangerous man, Christine.
We should all run.

John
Very dangerous.
So dangerous I am going for a shave.

John exits.

Julie
You have to help me.

Christine
I don't even understand you, let alone –

Julie
I'll tell you everything.

Christine

And with your bags packed.

Julie

I'll start at the beginning.

Christine

I don't care to hear the tale.
    Thank you.

Julie

But I can explain, I was caught by this horrible
moment of –

Christine

I'm not listening, Miss Julie. Can't you see?
    I am not listening to you any more.

Julie

What?

Beat.

Julie

What did you say?
    Christine?

Christine

Whatever happened last night is between you and him.
And God I suppose. Your immortal soul, but it goes no
further.
    Hush, I said. I am talking.
    I have had very little.
    In my life, Miss Julie, I have not had much.
    Except for him.
    Oh, I might not have had him like you have had
him, and you might pour scorn on what we had. But
there was a place in the universe where he was mine.
    And you who have everything. You. What, you
think you can take him as well?

Not while I am living.
I will stop you. I will put an end to it.

Julie

Come with us. Why don't you? I don't care.

Maybe the three of us could get further than two. John has this plan to run a hotel.

Christine

I know his plans.

Julie

So maybe we need a cook.

Beat.

Julie

Or maybe you aren't the cook.

Maybe you are the Lady and I am the cook. I don't care really, but to stay here is the end – Don't you see that? Come with us, as far as Glasgow anyway, and beyond that we'll see – where the mood takes us or where the trains lead. Ireland or America, why not, we could go to America. New York, where we could start all over, a little business, perhaps not the full hotel, but a bed and breakfast. Fancy that? Me in the office, John rustling up customers, and of course everyone wants to come and stay with us because we do the best breakfasts – not that you would cook them, no, we'd pay people to do that because you would be having far too good a time having your hair done and your nails and courting several men at once and all standing in queue to make you an offer of marriage, which of course you would turn down because you had your eye on an altogether different –

Christine

Do you even know when you are talking shit?

Julie
   Do I even . . . ?

Christine
   Yes.

Julie
   No.
      Not any more.

Christine turns to where John is standing.

Christine
   Did you really think to go?

John
   She had a notion.

Christine
   She said you had a notion.

John
   She is confused.

Christine
   She seems to have it all worked out in her scheming
   little mind.

John
   Don't use language like that.

Christine
   Why not?

John
   She is still your mistress.

Christine
   Hark at you.

John
   It is what you said to me, only moments ago. Don't
   tear it all down.

Christine

Ah, but I had respect for her then.

John

You are so above us all, aren't you? Sure it isn't Miss Julie that has the airs but the cook herself.

Christine

I have enough respect for myself to keep myself to myself. Yes. Unlike you.

John

God forbid that you should ever debase yourself. Ever risk anything. Ever show any emotion.

Christine

I thank my lucky stars. Particularly when it comes to thieves like you.

John

I didn't steal the daughter, she was freely given.

Christine

OK, what about the oats you sell under the table? Freely given too? The entire black market you have got going while the boss isn't looking?

John

You can talk –

You who takes a slice every time you go back to the same butcher. We're both lining our pockets, admit it. You as much as I.

Christine

A few pennies, John.

John

It adds up. I only mention it because you seem to be throwing the first stone.

Christine

At least I go to church. Confess my sins.

John
   Confess away.

Beat.

Christine
   I will not be damned, John.

John
   Neither will I.

Christine
   Good day, Miss.

Christine starts to go.

Christine
   Oh, and the strikers? The working class whose time is
   now? The strike is over. I just heard. The unions lost.
   And the workers have gone crawling for their jobs
   back. Every single one. Grown men begging, I heard.

John
   When?

Christine
   Last night. The Lord held out. He wouldn't budge and
   the union caved in. He's throwing them all off his land
   apparently, every one.

John
   I feel sick.

Christine
   It is how I said it would be. And as it has always been.

Beat.

Christine
   Don't think you can get away by car, by the way. As a
   precaution, I told the men on the gates not to let
   anyone past. I said the young miss wasn't herself and
   she must be kept in.

John

You witch.

Christine

I had to do something.

Good day to you both.

Christine leaves.

John

Damn her.

Take the money back, Julie.

Julie

I can't.

In order to make it look like it was forced, I bent the key.

John

So re-bend it.

Julie

It won't open.

Beat.

Julie

We'll get through the gates.

John

What? Past the men.

Julie

We'll give another order. They'll listen to me.

John

No. Not if she has said you are not yourself. We all know that phrase, we heard it too many times when it was said of your mother. And the men are too scared of the Lord to disobey.

She has made us a prison in this house.

Julie

So we will climb over the gates. We'll run.

John

On foot?
   And how far will we get?

Julie

As far as we can.

John

With your father only moments behind us? You'll trip
and stumble and be in the dirt. He'll catch us, Julie,
and what then? Either way he will never let you out of
the grounds again. He will say you are deranged like
your parent before you. He will not face the shame, so
he'll keep you in. Locked up. For ever if he has to.

Julie

Don't say that.

John

And me, who is to say what he will do to me?
   His favourite.

Beat.

Julie

So what do we do?

Beat.

John

What do we do? Or what do I do?

Julie

What do I do?

John

I wouldn't like to say.

Julie

But you have an idea.

John

Of sorts. Yes.

Julie walks away from him, caught in her own thoughts.

Julie

I won't be frightened, by the way.

Beat.

Julie

I am my mother's daughter. You tell me what is in your head.

Beat.

Julie

Just say it.
If there is a thought there, then let it out.

John

It was just a fleeting thing. A stupid notion that passed through. It's gone now.

Julie

You have to be brave. Apparently. To see it through. The worst is to start and change one's mind. Even my father couldn't do it, years ago when he tried. It's only my mother that has walked that path. How funny if both of us were able to do something he couldn't. Us women, braver than that shit.

John

I thought you loved him.

Julie

No.
Sorry. Never.
He fucked me up from the start. I was brought up not to trust anyone. Particularly men. And women, in fact maybe especially women. But whose fault, this whole mess? His? My mother's? Mine? God, there is nothing that is mine, not a thought that hasn't come

99

from my father, not a desire that wasn't passed down
to me from my mother, even this great all-humans-are-
equal notion – even that came from my wet fiancé.
Everything I am I have inherited from somewhere
along the line. So whose fault? Tell me? Which of all
those pieces leads to this? Or maybe it doesn't matter.
Maybe it is just as immaterial as the notion itself. For
after all, whoever's fault, it is me that bears the brunt.

John

Yes, but –

The bell rings.

Julie

He is back.

John

Christine will have passed him on the way to the
chapel.

Julie

Even if she hadn't spoken to him, the first place he will
have gone on his return is that little drawer, his fingers
searching for the key.

John picks up the phone.

John

It is John, Your Lordship.
        Yes, yes, right away. Of course I can . . . yes. Yes sir.

He puts the phone down.
He speaks to Julie.

John

He knows.

Julie

What did he say?

John

Nothing at all. His voice –

He asked for his boots, and his coffee.

As soon as I am able.

Julie

You're sure he knows?

John

I know how he is with those he means to punish.

I have heard that tone of voice when he talks of the mill.

The clipped vowels as he crushes a man's thumb between his forefingers.

Julie

Shit.

Fuck.

My head won't work, why won't it work? I know I have got to think quickly, more quickly, but I can't seem to do anything. Can't repent, can't run away, can't stay, can't live, can't die.

Help me.

Help me, John.

Tell me what to do. I won't argue.

You have the idea. You said you did. Make me do it.

John

If you can't make yourself –

Julie

I can't.

John

I can't help you.

Since the bell rang, I am my old self again, the spineless butler who does what he is told. If the boss were to come down here and tell me to slit my throat, oh, I could do that but –

Julie

So pretend you are the boss.

And I am the butler.
Could you play the role of my father?

John
No.

Julie
A hypnotist, then. You've been to the shows.

John nods.

Julie
And he says to the subject: get the broom.
And the man gets it.
He says sweep.
And the man sweeps.

John
But the subject has to be asleep.

Julie
I have been asleep for a long time.
There is nothing in the room but darkness and
shadows – and a man in black clothes and a high hat –
and your eyes glow like coals when the fire is going
out – and your face is a lump of white ashes.

*The sunlight has reached the floor and is now falling on
John.*

Julie
How warm and nice it is.

Julie rubs her hands as if warming them before a fire.

Julie
And so light, and so peaceful.

John takes the razor and puts it in her hands.

John
There's the broom. Go now, while it is light – to the
barn – and . . .

He whispers something in her ear.

Julie
But tell me none of this was my fault.
For none of it, will I be to blame.

John
Don't think about that.
Don't think about anything, don't think either of us will lose our nerve. What, already I am jumping at the thought of the bell ringing. Not the bell itself, but the hand behind it. And whatever the thought is behind the hand – cover up your ears, Julie.
It's ringing.
Ringing and ringing.
It won't stop and it won't stop, and it won't stop.

Two quick rings of the bell.

John
There is no other end to it.

She looks at him.
She takes out the razor.

Julie
What? Here?

John
I'll catch you if you fall.

The bell rings, again and again.
She unbuttons her dress.
She holds the blade to herself.

Julie
Promise?

John
Promise.

Blackout.